AF484674

Alexander Hamilton's Wish for Battlefield Glory

Written by C. Behrens

★ ★ ★

Illustrated by Bryan Werts

Independently Published

Author C. Behrens

Illustrations by Bryan Werts

Design by Kimberly Martin

ISBNs:
979-8-218-55625-9 (hardcover)
979-8-302-57218-9 (paperback)
979-8-218-55626-6 (eBook)

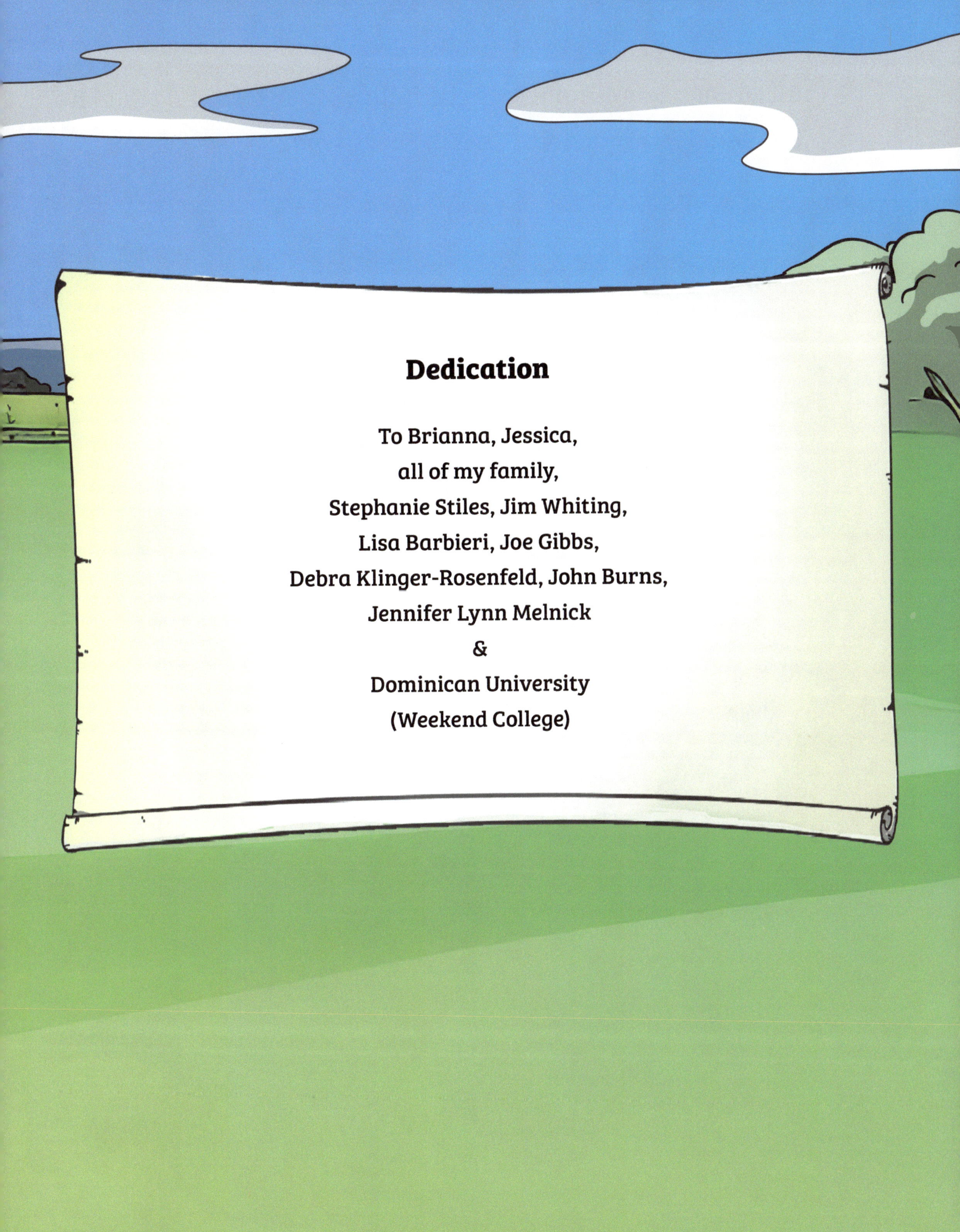

Dedication

To Brianna, Jessica,
all of my family,
Stephanie Stiles, Jim Whiting,
Lisa Barbieri, Joe Gibbs,
Debra Klinger-Rosenfeld, John Burns,
Jennifer Lynn Melnick
&
Dominican University
(Weekend College)

Alexander Hamilton wrote the following to a friend when he was fourteen years old, "I wish there was a WAR!"

A war would give him a chance to be a hero. Alexander thought becoming a hero would take away the shame of his father's desertion and the sadness of his mother's death. If he became a hero, he would no longer be just an unknown store clerk on the small Caribbean Island of St. Croix.

When Alexander was seventeen, a massive
hurricane swept through the Caribbean. He wrote
a vivid letter about the storm. It was published by
the Royal Danish American Gazette. His writing
impressed the island's governor and businessmen
so much that they offered to pay for him to attend
college in the American colonies. Alexander
accepted their offer.

Alexander entered King's College in New York in 1773. Rallies and riots against British rule were widespread at that time. Alexander became swept up in the revolutionary fervor and gave a strong speech on the school's campus in favor of freedom. In addition to his college subjects, he studied military texts.
NO!
King's College

The Revolutionary War began on April 19, 1775, in Lexington and Concord, Massachusetts. Alexander and his classmates formed a militia group called the Corsicans. They wore caps emblazoned with LIBERTY OR DEATH! They resolved to steal cannons from an abandoned British fort in New York. Despite heavy fire from a British warship anchored nearby, they succeeded in making off with twenty-one desperately needed cannons.

Alexander's bravado brought him offers to be an aide-de-camp to several generals, but he turned them all down. A desk job didn't interest him; it was the battlefield or bust! He accepted a position as an artillery captain. He trained his men, got them better uniforms, and even advanced them money if they needed it.

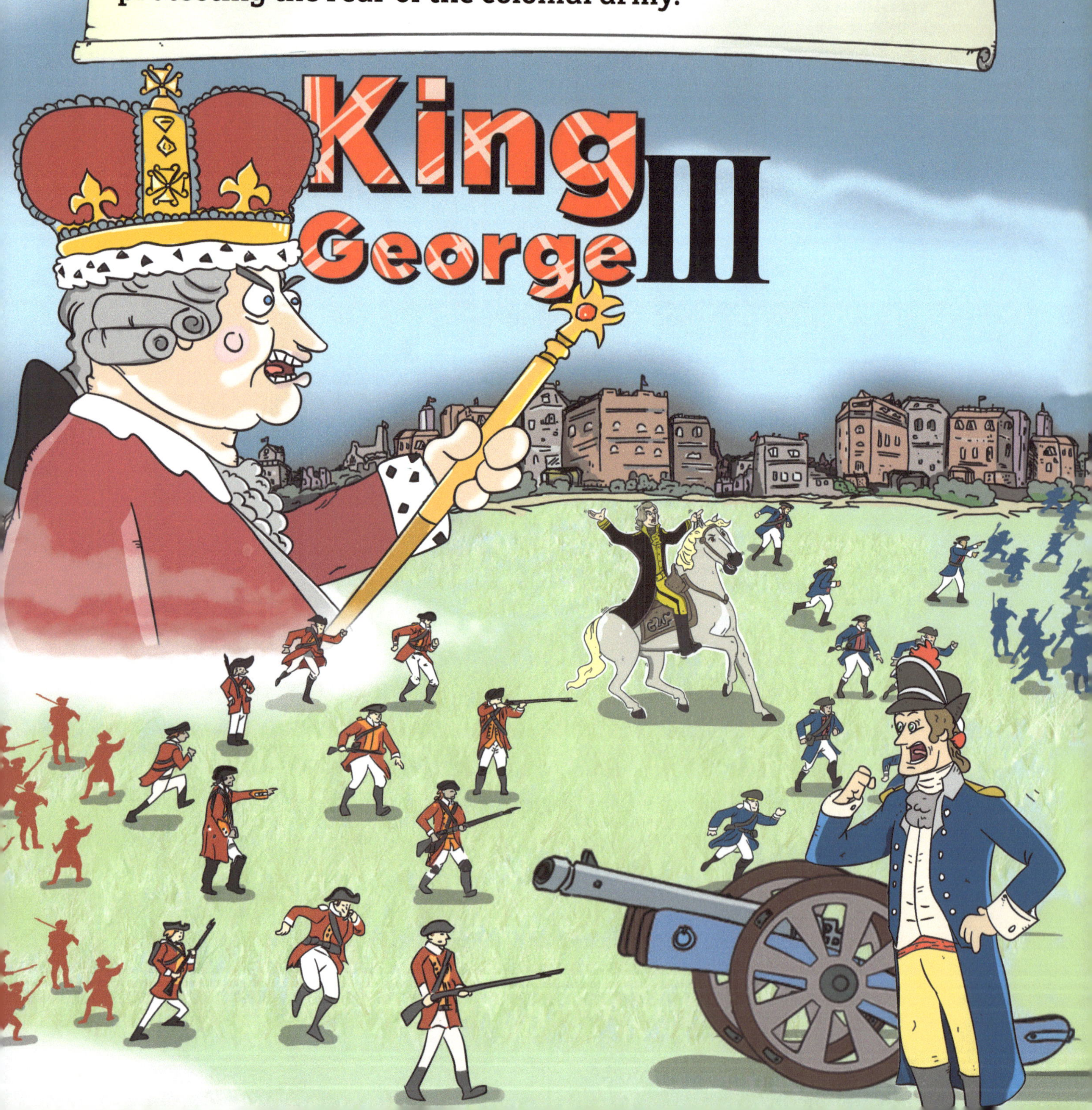

On July 2, 1776, the colonies declared their independence from British rule. King George III, who was the British king, sent an enormous army to New York to destroy the rebellion. The battle-hardened British soldiers easily overwhelmed George Washington's inexperienced troops. Washington and his men escaped with Alexander and a small group of troops protecting the rear of the colonial army.

Alexander soon found that most of warfare wasn't about being a hero. Washington's troops became tired and hungry as they retreated through New Jersey into Pennsylvania. They were worn down and miserable. Some didn't even have shoes. Morale had dropped considerably. Many of the soldiers became ill, including Alexander.

With defeat closing in, Washington planned a surprise attack against an enemy base in Trenton, New Jersey. It was garrisoned by about 1,000 Hessian troops who were fighting for the British. Although it was a cold and snowy night, Alexander forced himself out of his sickbed and resumed his command. Nothing would keep him from a chance at glory.

After General Washington led the depleted army across the icy Delaware River, his troops surrounded the enemy. Alexander and his small artillery unit dragged two cannons through the falling snow into position for the attack. On Alexander's command, his men opened fire. The Hessians were caught off guard on this Christmas night of 1776 and quickly surrendered. The successful sneak attack lifted the army's spirits and changed the tide of the war.

Aide-de-Camp

After the victory, Washington offered Alexander a job as his aide-de-camp. This time, Alexander accepted the offer. The position required him to solve disputes, award promotions, and deal with prisoner negotiations. In addition to those tasks, he ran errands and wrote letters for Washington.

Acquiring food and clothing were top priorities for Alexander, especially during the winter encampment of 1777-1778 at Valley Forge. The troops were hungry and cold. Alexander wrote letters to the states asking for food and supplies, but they refused to help. He quickly saw the need for a central government and a national bank that could support the army. This would eventually make him one of the most important figures in the future of the new nation.

Alexander was very busy as Washington's aide, but he never stopped yearning for a field command. The Battle of Monmouth on June 28, 1778, provided Alexander the opportunity he so desperately desired. One of his routine errands put him in the path of General Charles Lee and his men who were in the middle of a chaotic retreat from the British. Alexander stepped in and reasserted calm, telling Lee, "I will stay here with you, my dear General, and die with you!"

According to General Lee, Alexander appeared to be everywhere on the battlefield. He stopped another retreating infantry unit and ordered the men to fight back. The battle ended in a draw, but Alexander's courage and leadership impressed many of the soldiers.

Battle of Monmouth

Alexander returned to his duties as an aide to Washington, but he continually requested a field command. Washington denied his requests because he recognized Alexander's greatest strength was not on the battlefield. Alexander's best weapon was his mind and his vast knowledge of many things. Washington used Alexander's talents to train the troops, write letters, and speak to foreign officers who were assisting the colonial troops. Alexander even assisted with strategizing the colonial army's attacks. He was undeniably Washington's top aide. However, Alexander grew frustrated with his role and resigned from his staff position in February of 1781.

Although Alexander had left the army, he kept a close eye on the war. When he heard about Washington's plan to attack the British in Yorktown, Virginia, he hopped on his horse and galloped south to request a field command. Washington finally gave him the command of a light infantry battalion.

Redoubt 10

On the night of October 14, 1781, Alexander and his troops were ordered to attack a key outer British defensive position called Redoubt 10. It was during a moonless night, and Alexander wanted to use the element of surprise. He instructed his men to unload their guns and prepare their bayonets to avoid making any noise. Alexander led the way as they quietly and quickly encircled Redoubt 10. Then, on his command, the troops attacked. Within minutes, Alexander's men took control of the redoubt. The victory was fast and with very few casualties.

The victory at Yorktown, Virginia played a key role in forcing the British Army to surrender. It was the last major battle of the Revolution. Following the battle, Alexander praised others for the triumph. However, this was Alexander's long-awaited moment of glory. Just as he had wished ever since his childhood, the war made Alexander an American hero!

AUTHOR'S NOTE

What Alexander hadn't predicted was that he would not be remembered as a war hero, but as one of the Founding Fathers who built a new nation. He played a key role in the creation of the new U.S. Constitution and included his ideas for a strong central government. He increased the size of the army and created the Coast Guard. He assisted with founding the first national bank to establish credit for the new nation. He helped mint the U.S. currency and created the first coins: the dime, the penny, and the half penny! Since 1928, his portrait has been on the ten-dollar bill.

Alexander would have accomplished many other things, but he died after a duel with Aaron Burr. The duel took place on July 11, 1804. Three days later, all of New York City shut down for Alexander's funeral procession. Sidewalks and rooftops were packed with people trying to get a glimpse of his casket. After a somber service, he was laid to rest with full military honors at Trinity Church Cemetery. Sadly, he left behind a wife and seven children. His oldest son also died after a duel in 1801. Alexander was only forty-nine years old.

Works Consulted

Adler, David A., and Matt Collins. *A Picture Book of Alexander Hamilton.*

    Holiday House, 2019.

Brockenbrough, Martha. *Alexander Hamilton, Revolutionary.* Feiwel & Friends, 2017.

Brown, Don. *Aaron and Alexander.* Roaring Brook Press, 2015.

Chernow, Ron. *Alexander Hamilton.* Penguin Publishing Group, 2005.

Fritz, Jean. *Alexander Hamilton: The Outsider.* Penguin, 2011.

Kanefield, Teri. *Alexander Hamilton: The Making of America.*

    Abrams Books for Young Readers, 2017.

Kostyal, K. M. "Founding Fathers: America's Great Leaders and the Fight for

    Freedom." National Geographic Reissue 2020 from 2016. Print.

Norfolk Community Television (NCTV). "Alexander Hamilton, America's First Secretary

    of the Treasury Presented by Dr. Gary Hylander." *YouTube*, 11 Mar. 2014,

    www.youtube.com/watch?v=9cLtVzdZFrI. Accessed 15 Sept. 2024.

Schellhammer, Michael. Alexander Hamilton, Dangerous Man. Journal of the

    American Revolution. https://www.allthingsliberty.com, June 5, 2013. Web.

    August 2020.

Willard Sterne Randall. "Hamilton Takes Command." *Smithsonian*, Smithsonian.com,

    2003, www.smithsonianmag.com/history/hamilton-takes-command-74722445/.

    Accessed 5 Dec. 2019.

Alexander built this home for his family. He called it:
The Grange. It is now a museum in New York City.

C. Behrens is the author of the award-winning children's book, *Savanna's Treasure*, and an award-winning poem, *A Basketballer's Ditty!* Hard work and perseverance helped him graduate Magna Cum Laude from Dominican College in New York. He lives and works in New Jersey and has two beautiful daughters.

Bryan Werts is an illustrator, who for the past eight years has created vibrant characters and scenes for over seventy different children's titles. He holds a BS in Digital Design and Entertainment and lives in Louisville, Kentucky with his wife and son.